Dragon Boats in August
NYC through a YEAR of CELEBRATIONS

D1518668

John Ewing

Published by QueensBooks.NYC, LLC

For Logan & Amelia,
who make every day a CELEBRATION

Dedicated to José Oswaldo Gómez

Celebrations

happen every day in New York City. They can last a few hours, a week, or even a month. Some are big parades for everyone to enjoy. Others are quietly observed by families at home.

Many celebrations occur on a particular date on the Gregorian calendar. Just as many vary year to year, like Passover on the Jewish calendar or Eid al-Fitr on the Islamic calendar. And some are timed with the seasons, or the movements of the sun and moon.

There are holidays with music and dances, special foods, symbolic objects, rituals, or decorations and costumes. Some recall legends that are thousands of years old. Other celebrations honor recent events in the memories of people you know.

There are as many celebrations as there are cultures in the world—all are welcome here. What do they share? All are creative, filled with imagination, stories, and wonder. And celebrations are repeated, year after year, to keep their meanings alive.

This book contains just a few. Can you name other celebrations in your community? Think about the traditions and special memories they preserve—and make new every year.

Let's CELEBRATE!

Dragon Boats in August
Flushing Meadows Corona Park
QUEENS

HONG KONG

We put on
our vests and step
into the Dragon Boat.

"PADDLES UP!"
... reach catch pull exit ...

We move as a team, matching the
drummer's beat. We glide over the lake,
making friends with the water spirits,
sunlight sparkling silver   on
the Unisphere.

Like ripples on water,
a Chinese legend
has traveled
thousands of miles
from Hong Kong to festivals
around the world
... to **Queens,
NYC!**

Feathers in September
West Indian Day Parade
Crown Heights, BROOKLYN

On Labor Day,
we dress up
like Birds of Paradise
in colors of the Caribbean.

Flags fly from Trinidad,
Jamaica, Haiti, Aruba, Grenada
... names with rhythm and music,
the sounds of Carnival, of home.

For months, we've sewn sequins
on costumes. Our feather fans and
headdresses wave as we dance
to calypso and soca.

The parade becomes a party.
We make Eastern Parkway
an island fantasy
for a day.

Inspired by a legend, **Dragon Boat** races were first organized by **Chinese** farmers and fishermen thousands of years ago and are still popular in Hong Kong today.

Around the world, communities of Chinese immigrants and their descendants—like in **Flushing, Queens**—celebrate the Dragon Boat race as a symbol of heroism, teamwork, and community spirit.

With carved figurehead, tail, and painted scales, the Dragon Boat is "brought to life" by touching each eye with a dot of fresh red paint.

Celebrating New York's version of **Carnival**, the **West Indian Day Parade** draws millions of participants and spectators to **Crown Heights, Brooklyn,** on Labor Day.

Fantastic costumes of feathers, beads, face paint, and masks recall the birds, flowers, and history of island life, as **calypso** and **soca** music and dancing bring a burst of creative expression to the streets.

In the **West Indies** and in Brooklyn, this **Afro-Caribbean** holiday begins with **J'ouvert**, an all-night party that sets the stage for Carnival.

9

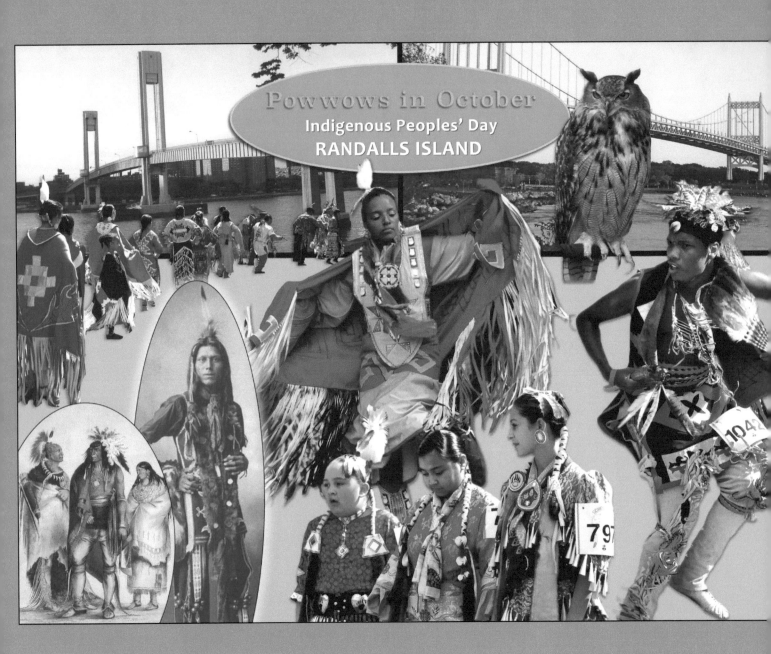

Powwows in October
Indigenous Peoples' Day
RANDALLS ISLAND

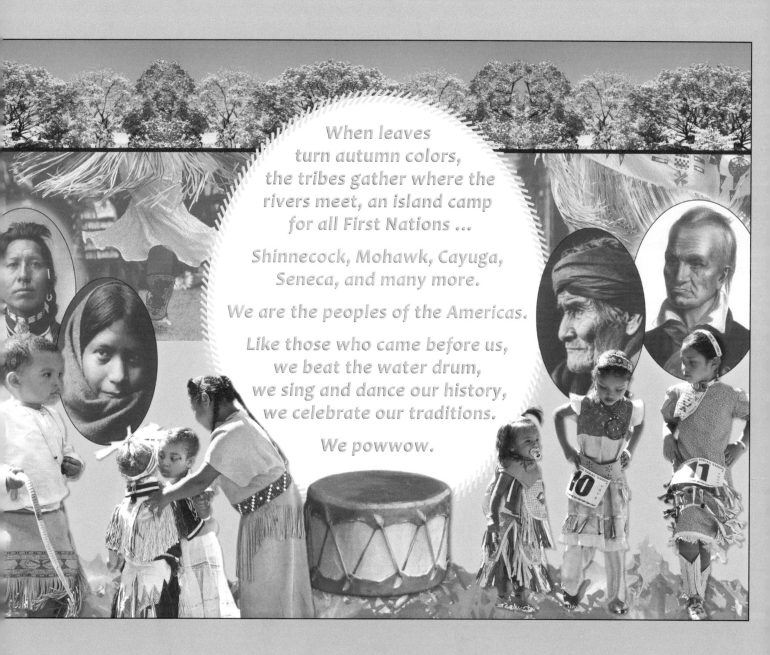

When leaves
turn autumn colors,
the tribes gather where the
rivers meet, an island camp
for all First Nations ...

Shinnecock, Mohawk, Cayuga,
Seneca, and many more.

We are the peoples of the Americas.

Like those who came before us,
we beat the water drum,
we sing and dance our history,
we celebrate our traditions.

We powwow.

Balloons in November

Thanksgiving Day Parade

MANHATTAN

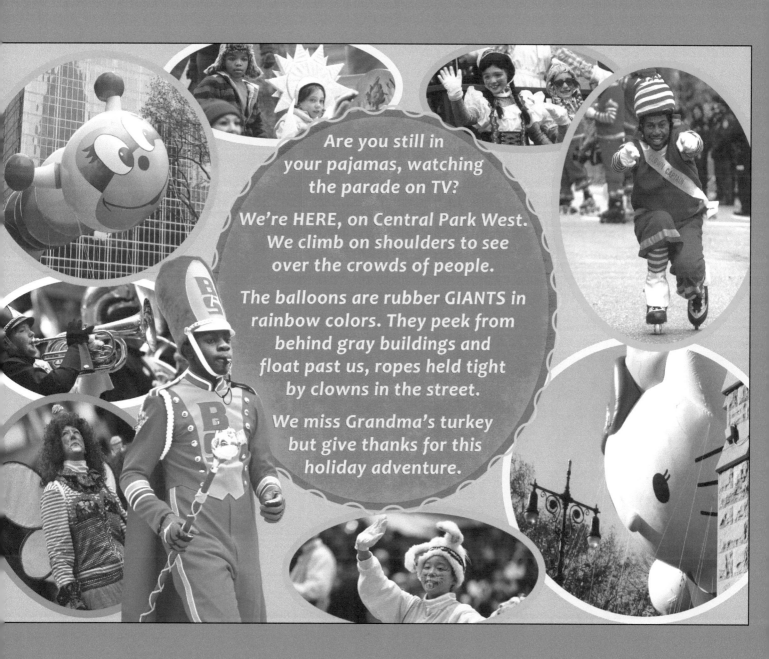

Are you still in
your pajamas, watching
the parade on TV?

We're HERE, on Central Park West.
We climb on shoulders to see
over the crowds of people.

The balloons are rubber GIANTS in
rainbow colors. They peek from
behind gray buildings and
float past us, ropes held tight
by clowns in the street.

We miss Grandma's turkey
but give thanks for this
holiday adventure.

Before European conquest, the Americas were inhabited by thousands of indigenous tribal nations—from the **Inuit** of the Arctic to the **Onawo** of Patagonia.

Indigenous Peoples' Day celebrates **First Peoples** and honors their histories and cultures. These communal **powwows** include traditional dances, ceremonial costumes, arts, and crafts.

There are dozens of tribes in New York State alone, and the powwow on Randalls Island— organized by the **Redhawk Native American Arts Council**—is one of the largest.

Since 1924, **Macy's** department store has sponsored a **Thanksgiving Day Parade** beloved by generations of Americans, who attend the event in person or watch on TV.

The parade's spectacular polyurethane balloons—including storybook characters, cartoons, and **Santa Claus**—delight the crowds, who arrive in the early morning hours to fill the sidewalks along **Central Park**.

Many bring blankets and hot chocolate. Another fun tradition is to watch the inflating of the balloons on **Thanksgiving Eve**.

Dreidels in December

❄ Hanukkah ❄

NEW YORK CITY

"Dreidel,
dreidel, dreidel ... "

We sing and spin the top,
Chanukah gelt for you and me.

For eight nights, we celebrate
the Festival of Lights,
a new candle lit each evening.
The menorah reminds us of the
oil lamp that never burns out.

In the longest nights of winter,
we gather family and friends
around a table blessed with
warmth and light.

Camels in January
Three Kings' Day Parade
EAST HARLEM ♛ El Barrio

We put on
paper crowns and
our winter coats
to celebrate
El Día de los Tres Reyes Magos

... three wise kings from afar,
three camels up Lexington Avenue.

We shake cardboard maracas
and sing parrandas de Navidad,
gifts to the newborn baby,

a surprise of love
to the world.

Epiphany!

During winter's longest nights, **Hanukkah** is a warm and joyous **Festival of Lights** shared with family and friends.

The eight-night holiday celebrated by Jews around the world has beloved traditions, including lighting the **menorah** candles, eating potato **latkes**, exchanging gifts like **Chanukah gelt** (chocolate coins), and spinning the **dreidel.**

The toy top is stamped with **Hebrew** letters honoring the ancient miracle of the oil lamp that never burns out. In olden times, dreidels were made of clay.

CHABAD OF REGO PARK
Wishes You a...
Happy Chanukah!

Dreidel, dreidel, dreidel ...

The **Nativity** tells the story of the journey of three wise kings
to bestow gifts upon the infant **Jesus**.

Epiphany, the **Christian** feast day honoring this event, is beloved in
Puerto Rico and throughout Latin America as **El Día de los Tres Reyes Magos,**
celebrated with processions, carols, paper crowns, rattles, and
Roscón de Reyes, a special bread baked with a tiny figurine inside as a lucky surprise.

In exchange for gifts, children leave shoebox mangers of grass beneath their beds
for the weary camels.

Red Lanterns in February
Lunar New Year
Chinatown, MANHATTAN

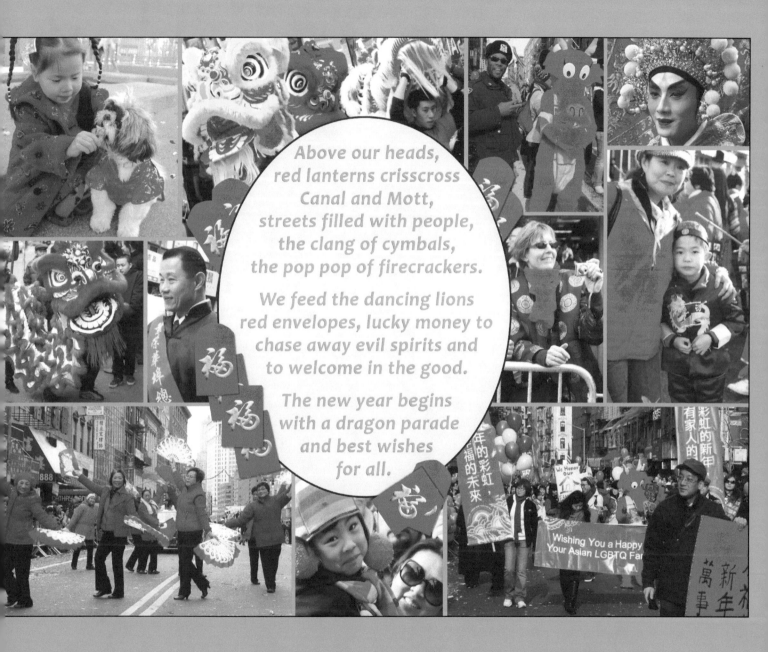

Above our heads,
red lanterns crisscross
Canal and Mott,
streets filled with people,
the clang of cymbals,
the pop pop of firecrackers.

We feed the dancing lions
red envelopes, lucky money to
chase away evil spirits and
to welcome in the good.

The new year begins
with a dragon parade
and best wishes
for all.

Colors in March
Holi ✸ Phagwah
Richmond Hill, QUEENS

24

A toss of abir,
a game of tag ...

March makes a mark on
hands, faces, and nature too.

We celebrate the end of winter
with a festival of Colors.

Sweet treats for eyes, ears,
and tasting, all is new.

We play in perfumed showers
from earth and sky,
from Krishna and Radha.

Nothing may
offend the senses,

Holi Hai!

Lunar New Year, China's principal holiday, is celebrated
around the world by East Asian immigrants and their descendants,
especially in New York's Chinatown and Flushing communities.

Families and neighbors exchange wishes of health, happiness, and prosperity
symbolized by red envelopes with small sums of money.

For fun, children feed red envelopes to costumed lions,
who dance door to door, carrying good luck down the street.
The holiday culminates with a Lantern Festival.

The **Hindu** holiday of **Holi**—or **Phagwah**, in communities of
Indo-Caribbean immigrants and their descendants like in **Richmond Hill**, **Queens**—
celebrates the triumph of good over evil, spring over winter,
new crops, and renewed relationships.

Symbolized with a **Festival of Colors**, the season is celebrated
with dance and music, sweets, and playful games.

The highlight of Holi, for young and old alike, is a game of tag in a
rainbow shower of **abir**—colored and scented talcum powder.

Cherry Blossoms in April
Sakura Matsuri
BROOKLYN Botanic Garden

The cherry
trees will bloom
when they bloom ...
Springtime is a mystery.
We cheer when it arrives.
Hanami!

We meet with family and friends,
make a picnic in the garden,
dance barefoot on new grass.

The beauty of spring is
here and gone in a wink.
We celebrate nature
with our eyes and
imagination.

Fiestas in May
Cinco de Mayo
NEW YORK CITY

Mexico is far
from New York City.
Fiestas help us to remember
where we come from.

On Cinco de Mayo, we are
Poblanos. We remember Puebla.
We share the pride of our city
y la cultura mexicana.

When we sing rancheras,
eat chiles en nogada, or dress
and dance as Chinelos,
we think of home.

STATION DE PUEBLA. ESTACION DE PUEBLA. STATION OF PUEBLA.

Inauguracion del camino de fierro

In **Japan**, cherry blossoms, or **sakura**, symbolize
the beauty and impermanence of life.

Enjoying springtime flowers is a Japanese tradition called **hanami**.
Outside of Japan, cherry-blossom festivals—**sakura matsuri**—have sprung up
around groves of cherry trees, such as in **Washington, DC**, or at
the **Brooklyn Botanic Garden**.

Japanese arts and culture are celebrated in performances,
community activities, or just dressing up—
a fun tradition for NYC fans of Japanese **anime** and **cosplay**.

Outside of **Puebla, Mexico,** few know the significance of **Cinco de Mayo**—
the date in 1862 when the Mexican army defeated French occupation.

While many in the U.S. view this holiday as just a good reason for a party,
New York is home to nearly half a million **Poblanos**—
immigrants from Puebla—who celebrate **fiestas** as a way to preserve
their ties to home through traditional songs, foods, dances, and costumes.

Local Poblano groups have also revived the ceremonial arts of
their pre-Hispanic **Mixtec** heritage.

When days
are long and sunny,
sea creatures swim up
from the deep or ride down
on the train, costumed for a
Brooklyn boardwalk parade.

We celebrate Summer Solstice
in homemade fins and
feather boas, a tribute to
aquatic life and free expression.

Shake a tambourine, shake a
flipper ... be creative!
We have surfside fun
on Coney Island.

Fireworks in July
Independence Day
U.S.A.

BOOM!
A burst of color
lights up the night sky,
a plume of smoke,
reflections on rippling water,
and smiles on a million faces.

On the Fourth of July,
we come from every borough,
from around the world,
to watch holiday fireworks
and celebrate on the riverbank.

Together we say,
HAPPY BIRTHDAY
USA!

Summer officially begins in New York with the **Coney Island Mermaid Parade**, a celebration of the **Summer Solstice**, creative fun, and community spirit.

Homemade costumes and floats bring to life mermaids, sea creatures, sailors, and pirates in a festive boardwalk procession, as nearby beachgoers return to the sun and surf of the **Atlantic Ocean.**

Founded in 1983, this DIY art parade is now a **Brooklyn** tradition, like cotton candy, the **Wonder Wheel**, and **Nathan's Famous** hot dogs.

Independence Day—or **Fourth of July**—celebrates the United States of America's independence from Britain, declared in 1776.

The **USA**'s national anthem, "The Star-Spangled Banner," speaks of **"the rockets' red glare,"** a symbol of freedom that we commemorate in spectacular **fireworks** displays across the country.

All of NYC comes together on **July 4th** to celebrate the nation's birthday, gathering on the banks of the **East River** or **Hudson River** to look up and enjoy the show.

39

Acknowledgments

Special thanks to Jil Picariello, Nomi Schwarzbaum, David Ewing, Teri Kusenberger Ewing, Marsha Ewing Och and family, Cynthia Ewing Brevell, and Charles Ewing for feedback on early drafts.

Credits

Dragon Boats in August: NYC through a Year of Celebrations features photography made available under Creative Commons license. Images were researched independently, and subjects bear no known relation to each other, the photographers, publisher, or author. QueensBooks.NYC thanks the following photographers for their creativity and generosity - for links to their work, go to www.queensbooks.nyc/dbia-credits:

Cover, Title & Dedication Pages - Sharon Chapman, Nick Hubbard, Diallo Jamal & Paul Stein

 Dragon Boats in August

Chris Goldberg

Nick Hubbard

Diallo Jamal

Chauncey Mellows

Sam Sith

Rob Young

Michael Zanussi

Feathers in September

Carnaval.com Studios

Neil Gibbs

Joe Mazzola

Thomas Jefferys
New York Public Library

Paul Stein

 Balloons in November

Anthony Quintano

Sharon Chapman

Kurt Wagoner
permission pending

Powwows in October

Jana Apergis

Raphael Bieber

George Catlin
Yale University Art Gallery

Geronimo, Edward Curtis
New York Public Library

Pakit, Maracopa girl, Edward Curtis
New York Public Library

John Ewing

Seneca chief, Charles Bird King
New York Public Library

Pete Mitchell (Dustmaker), F. A. Rinehart
New York Public Library

Thunder Cloud, Blackfeet, F. A. Rinehart
New York Public Library

Carlos A. Smith

We love feedback!

Please post a review at the retailer where you purchased this book.

Thank You

Dreidels in December

Jeffrey Bary

Selena Beckman-Harned

Joshua Bousel
permission pending

CCAC North Library

Sharon Chapman

Phil Davis

Danny Flam & The Maccabeats
permission pending

Joe Goldberg

Chajm Guski

Amy Guth

Andrea Moed

Arturo Pardavila III

Paurian

Chris Pounds

Marina Shemesh

Shoshanah

John Hollingsworth &
Staccabees

Camels in January

Dave Bledsoe
FreeVerse Photography

"Chameaux au désert"
Schroeder & Cie
New York Public Library

Internet Archive Book Images

Colors in March

Dave Bledsoe
FreeVerse Photography

Roup Hardowar

Joe Mazzola

Red Lanterns in February

Dom Crossley

John Gillespie

Ben Grantham

Patrick Kwan

Joe Mazzola

Pranavian

Ed Schipul

May S. Young

Cherry Blossoms in April

C. Fagel

Kano School
Yale University Art Gallery

Eric Lee

New York Public Library

Samit Sarkar

Carlos A. Smith

May S. Young

Harumi Yukawa

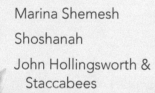

Fiestas in May

Bunky's Pickle

C. Castro
New York Public Library

Memorial Student Center, A&M University

Kathryn Prybylski

Paul Sableman

Ildar Sibgatullin
permission pending

Paul Stein

Christian Ramiro González Verón

Mermaids in June

Boston Public Library

Alex Martinez

Eugene Peretz

Teri Tynes

Tredok (Pierre Angot)

Fireworks in July

Eric Fleming

Matt Joyce

Jiunn Kang Too

M Yashna

Mamojo

Alex Martinez

Philippe Put

Anthony Quintano

Harsha K R

Sio

Book Design by **John Ewing**

QueensBooks.NYC

QUEENS is the largest of New York City's five boroughs, and the most diverse community in the United States. More than 135 languages are spoken in Queens, and people emigrate from countries around the globe to make Queens their home.

QueensBooks.NYC was founded to share stories and customs from around the world with young readers everywhere. We also tell stories from the rich cultural tapestry of NYC. For new and upcoming titles, visit QueensBooks.NYC.

QueensBooks are designed to meet New York State Learning & Common Core Standards.

Also available in Enhanced Multi-Touch  &

Join our email list at QueensBooks.NYC & follow us on

A WORLD OF STORIES
2017

CPSIA information can be obtained
at www.ICGtesting.com
Printed in the USA
LVHW070134230920
666820LV00010B/513